THE GAMBIA 2016 HUMAN RIGHTS REPORT

EXECUTIVE SUMMARY

The Gambia's constitution enumerates a full range of provisions and assurances for a multiparty democratic republic. Human rights organizations and opposition parties, however, claimed the government repeatedly took steps to restrict the democratic space. In 2011 voters reelected President Yahya Jammeh to a fourth term in a peaceful, orderly election; however, international observers considered it neither free nor fair. President Jammeh's party, the Alliance for Patriotic Reorientation and Construction (APRC), continued to dominate the political landscape, winning an overwhelming majority of national assembly seats in the parliamentary elections in 2012 and local assembly seats in local elections in 2013. Six of the seven opposition parties boycotted or otherwise did not participate in both the National Assembly and local government elections to protest government intervention and intimidation of opponents.

Civilian authorities at times did not maintain effective control over the security forces. The regime responded with excessive force to peaceful public protests on April 14, April 16, and May 9. More than 70 supporters of the United Democratic Party (UDP) were arrested; several were beaten and tortured during the three protests. Thirty of the detainees were convicted on July 20 and July 21, and sentenced to three years' imprisonment. Two of the detainees died in custody.

During a period of political crisis, President Jammeh first accepted, and then rejected, the results of a December 1 presidential election in which he was defeated by Adama Barrow, the candidate of a coalition of opposition parties, in what international observers assessed to be a fair and democratic vote. On December 9, Jammeh declared that a new election would be conducted, and during the month he authorized three petitions challenging the election results in the Supreme Court. Jammeh refused to leave power despite visits by the UN special representative of the secretary general for West Africa and the Sahel and two high-level Economic Community of West African States (ECOWAS) negotiating teams. Several individuals wearing T-shirts with the slogan "#Gambia has decided" were arrested between December 9 and the end of the year. The military occupied the headquarters of the Independent Electoral Commission on December 13. In December Jammeh also refused the requests of several local religious, professional, nongovernmental, and civil society organizations that he hand over power peacefully to President-elect Barrow.

The most serious human rights abuses reported included torture, arbitrary arrest, and prolonged pretrial and incommunicado detention; enforced disappearances of citizens; and government harassment and abuse of its critics. Officials routinely used various methods of intimidation to retain power.

Other reported human rights abuses included a corrupt and inefficient judiciary; poor prison conditions; denial of due process; restrictions on privacy and freedoms of speech, press, and assembly; corruption; violence against women and girls, including female genital mutilation/cutting (FGM/C); early and forced marriage; trafficking in persons, including child prostitution; discrimination against lesbian, gay, bisexual, transgender, and intersex individuals; and child labor.

The government enacted laws banning FGM/C and early and forced marriage and took steps to prosecute or punish some individuals who committed abuses. Nevertheless, impunity and the lack of consistent enforcement remained problems.

Section 1. Respect for the Integrity of the Person, Including Freedom from:

a. Arbitrary Deprivation of Life and other Unlawful or Politically Motivated Killings

There were several reports the government or its agents committed arbitrary or unlawful killings. On June 16, the government confirmed that UDP Organizing Secretary Ebrima Solo Sandeng died while in police custody. On April 14, Sandeng was arrested and reportedly tortured to death by members of the National Intelligence Agency (NIA) for leading a peaceful protest demanding "proper electoral reform." Nogoi Njie, one of the incarcerated protesters, said she saw Sandeng at NIA headquarters on April 14 "completely naked, flat on the ground, badly beaten, his body swollen, and bleeding profusely." After defense lawyers demanded to know Sandeng's whereabouts during court proceedings, the prosecution acknowledged that Sandeng had died. The prosecution's admission followed the president's interview with weekly news magazine *Jeune Afrique* on June 14, in which he admitted to Sandeng's death, claiming that it is "very common" for people to die in detention or during interrogation. UDP deputy chairman of the Sandu Darsilami constituency, Ibrima Solo Krummah, reportedly died in state custody on August 20. UDP members claimed that Krummah, who was arrested on May 9, along with several other UDP members, was tortured, and denied medical treatment. The government, however, stated that Krummah was receiving medical treatment and died of natural causes.

b. Disappearance

There were reports of politically motivated disappearances during the year. Men in civilian clothes reportedly abducted Sanusi Sanyang, a UDP supporter, a few days after peaceful protests organized by UDP supporters on April 14 and April 16. In 2013, two individuals of U.S.-Gambian dual nationality, Alhagie Ceesay and Ebrima Jobe, disappeared after last being seen in the country. In 2014 the attorney general stated the government had begun an investigation into the disappearances. There were no updates by year's end.

c. Torture and Other Cruel, Inhuman, or Degrading Treatment or Punishment

The constitution and law prohibit such practices; however, there were reports security forces tortured, beat, and mistreated persons in custody. Police arrested three men on May 11 and charged them with sedition after they allegedly said in a private conversation overheard by a government official the president disliked the Mandinka ethnic group. On June 21, defense counsel Abdoulie Fatty contested the admissibility of the defendants' statements, alleging that his clients had been physically and psychologically tortured, threatened with electric shock, and held at gunpoint to compel them to sign statements of guilt written by the police. On June 29, the magistrate ordered the suspects to testify and to narrate the circumstances under which their statements were given. The case remained underway at year's end.

In 2014 the government prevented UN special rapporteurs from investigating reports of torture and extrajudicial execution, having initially permitted them to conduct this investigation. The team's preliminary findings indicated the NIA consistently practiced torture. Police reportedly tortured individuals suspected of common crimes. The UN findings indicated the NIA tortured detainees for days or weeks; methods included severe beatings, electric shock, asphyxiation, and burning. According to Human Rights Watch, methods also included water torture, rape, and simulated burial.

Security officers arrested opposition activist Nogoi Njie on April 14 for taking part in an unauthorized' protest. In a May 11 affidavit, Njie specified how she and her codetainees were abused by the NIA at its Banjul headquarters. Nogoi stated she was handcuffed and beaten with hoses and batons while water was poured over her and that she was threatened with death.

During the year there were no known prosecutions in civil or military courts of security force members accused of mistreating individuals. The 2001 Indemnity Act gives the president authority to prevent the prosecution of security force members for acts committed during a "state of emergency" or an "unlawful assembly."

Prison and Detention Center Conditions

Prison conditions were harsh and potentially life threatening due to food shortages, gross overcrowding, physical abuse, and inadequate sanitary conditions and medical care.

Physical Conditions: Prison cells were overcrowded, damp, and poorly ventilated. Inmates complained of poor sanitation and food, and occasionally of having to sleep on the floor. One prisoner reported that she was held in a cell that often experienced total darkness for long periods at night and was often subject to electrical shocks due to faulty wiring in the cell, a situation that was not addressed. Officials allowed detainees to receive food from the outside prior to conviction, but required convicted inmates to eat only meals supplied by the prisons. Medical facilities in prisons were poor, and authorities sent sick inmates to a hospital in Banjul or nearby health centers for examination and treatment. Former inmates and human rights nongovernmental organizations (NGOs) reported a high prisoner-mortality rate. Reports indicated prisoners died of neglect or lack of access to health care. During the summer, temperatures in cells became extremely high, and there were no measures to reduce heat. Authorities at the NIA held most detainees in solitary confinement and often in dark, rat- and insect-infested rooms.

In 2015 Mile 2 Prison, which has an intended capacity of 450 inmates, held 536 prisoners and detainees, including six women.

Administration: Officials generally allowed inmates to have visits, with the exception of political inmates, who reportedly were denied access to lawyers and family members.

Authorities sometimes investigated credible allegations of inhumane conditions. A Prisons Visiting Committee, which included representatives of several government agencies, is empowered to monitor prison conditions. Former minister of interior Ousman Sonko stated that the committee visited the central prison weekly and submitted reports on substandard conditions.

The Office of the Ombudsman can investigate all complaints submitted to it, including those concerning bail conditions, pretrial detention, and confinement of juvenile offenders.

<u>Independent Monitoring</u>: The government did not permit the International Committee of the Red Cross or media access to monitor prison conditions. While local NGOs and diplomatic missions assisted prisoners, authorities did not allow them to monitor conditions.

In 2014 the government invited UN special rapporteurs investigating reports of torture and extrajudicial execution to visit. The government, however, canceled the invitation without explanation in August 2014 and rescheduled it for November 2014. After the UN special rapporteur team arrived, the government denied it access to the security wing of Mile 2 Prison, violating the agreed upon terms of reference. Consequently, the rapporteurs could not complete the full mandate of the mission.

d. Arbitrary Arrest or Detention

The constitution and law prohibit arbitrary arrest and detention and stipulate that authorities must charge or release any person arrested by police or other security agencies within 72 hours. There were, however, numerous instances of police and other security force members' arbitrarily arresting and detaining citizens longer than 72 hours without formally charging them.

There were multiple examples of arbitrary arrest or detention similar to the following: On September 1, Momodou Sarjo Jallow was dismissed from his August 23 appointment as deputy minister of foreign affairs and arrested on September 2. On October 7, the *Point* newspaper reported that Jallow was represented by Senior Defense Counsel Antouman Gaye in proceedings at the Banjul Special Criminal Court, and that Jallow had been held by the NIA. While the authorities did not admit that Jallow was in NIA custody and Jallow never appeared in court, Justice Ottaba ruled on October 17 that Jallow should be granted bail in the sum of 200,000 dalasi ($4,550), with a property of the like sum, and two Gambian sureties.

Role of the Police and Security Apparatus

The Gambia Armed Forces are responsible for external defense and serve under the authority of the minister of defense, a position held by the president. Police, under the Ministry of the Interior, are responsible for public security. The NIA, which reports directly to the president, is responsible for protecting state security, collecting intelligence, and conducting covert investigations. The law does not authorize the NIA to investigate police abuses, but the NIA often assumed police functions such as detaining and questioning criminal suspects. The Department of Immigration, under the Ministry of the Interior, is responsible for migration and border control.

Security force members frequently were corrupt and ineffective. Impunity was a problem, and police sometimes defied court orders.

The prosecution and legal affairs unit of the Gambia Police Force has two officers assigned to human rights issues, but they stated they received no complaints of abuses committed by police officers during the year. Observers believed citizens avoided reporting abuses to the unit due to fear of reprisal, lack of substantive redress, and a general mistrust of police. The Office of the Ombudsman appeared to handle most complaints against police officers (see section 5).

Arrest Procedures and Treatment of Detainees

The law requires authorities to obtain a warrant before arresting a person, but police and NIA officers often arrested individuals without a warrant. Periods of detention generally ranged from a few to 72 hours, the legal limit after which authorities must charge or release detainees; however, there were numerous instances of detentions exceeding the 72-hour limit. Authorities generally did not inform detainees promptly of charges against them. There was a functioning bail system; however, prosecutors customarily opposed even applications for bail for detainees charged with misdemeanors and ordered lengthy adjournments to allow additional time to prepare their cases. Judges and magistrates sometimes set bail at unreasonably high amounts. Courts occasionally released accused offenders on bail only to have law enforcement personnel rearrest them as they were leaving court, sometimes to provide the prosecution more time to prepare cases.

In 2014 authorities reportedly arrested Seedy Jaiteh, human resources director of the state-owned telecommunications company GAMTEL, at his residence and drove him away in an unmarked car with tinted windows. Media reported authorities did not allow family members and lawyers access to him. He remained in detention at year's end.

Officials did not allow detainees prompt access to a lawyer or family members, although officials generally allowed convicted prisoners to meet privately with an attorney. The judiciary provided only those indigent persons accused of murder or manslaughter with lawyers at public expense.

Military decrees enacted prior to the adoption of the constitution in 1997 give the NIA and the interior minister broad powers to detain individuals indefinitely without charge "in the interest of national security." These detention decrees are inconsistent with the constitution but have not been legally challenged. The government claimed it no longer enforced the decrees, but such detentions continued to occur.

On April 27, defense lawyer Antouman Gaye, and his cocounsel, representing Ousainou Darboe, leader of the opposition UDP, told the Banjul High Court that "authorities have ignored the court's order to grant the accused persons access to lawyers, family members, medical attention, and receive food from their family members."

Arbitrary Arrest: Security forces arbitrarily arrested citizens routinely during the year (see sections 1.e., 2.a., and 5). In 2014 the president dismissed newly appointed Minister of Education Momodou Sabally, and he was held for 41 days by the NIA without charge. He was subsequently charged with abuse of office while serving in the presidential administration and held for approximately five months before being released on bail pending trial. The government dropped the charges without explanation in September.

On January 27, *Foroyaa* newspaper reported 30 female police and military personnel were arbitrarily detained at the Yundum Police Station and at Fajara Training School, on suspicion of skin bleaching, which President Jammeh banned in September 2015. The female detainees were released without charge or court appearance on February 2.

Pretrial Detention: Backlogs and inefficiency in the justice system resulted in lengthy pretrial detention. In 2015 approximately 30 percent of inmates in the prison system were in pretrial detention; some had been incarcerated for several years awaiting trial.

The executive branch interfered in cases before the court; judges and magistrates routinely ignored or summarily dismissed a defendant's challenge to arbitrary detention. In those cases where the court responded positively to legal objections to arbitrary arrests, the state invariably ignored the courts' rulings.

Detainee's Ability to Challenge Lawfulness of Detention before a Court: Persons arrested or detained, regardless of whether on criminal or other grounds, may challenge in court the legal basis or arbitrary nature of their detention, but successful challenges are rare.

Amnesty: In 2015 the president pardoned 256 convicted prisoners and detainees, including several political prisoners. The president expanded this amnesty to include 12 detained family members of persons suspected of involvement in the failed coup of December 2014. The convicts included 53 foreigners; all were subsequently deported or allowed to leave.

e. Denial of Fair Public Trial

The constitution provides for an independent judiciary; however, the courts lacked independence, and corruption among judges and attorneys was reportedly common. Amnesty International noted the president's power to remove a judge, nominally in consultation with the Judicial Service Commission, interfered with judicial independence. Judges presiding over "sensitive" cases who made decisions not considered favorable to the government risked dismissal.

There was little stability in senior judiciary positions; for example, Magistrate Omar Jabang was dismissed and arrested on May 3, allegedly for acquitting and discharging a businessman, Yusupha Saidy. Jabang was reinstated after a two-day detention at Police Headquarters in Banjul and continued to preside over cases.

Frequent delays and missing or unavailable witnesses, judges, and lawyers often impeded trials. Many cases were delayed because of adjournments to allow police or the NIA more time to continue their investigations.

To alleviate the backlog, the government continued to recruit judges and magistrates from Commonwealth countries, especially Nigeria, with similar legal systems. Authorities particularly subjected foreign magistrates and judges, who often presided over sensitive cases, to executive pressure.

Trial Procedures

The law provides for the presumption of innocence, a fair and public trial without undue delay, adequate time and facilities to prepare a defense, and the right of appeal. Officials, however, generally did not properly inform defendants of the charges against them. Officials provided interpretation into defendants' local languages as necessary without cost from the moment charged through all appeals. By law no one may be compelled to testify or confess guilt. Trials generally were open to the public, unless closed-court sessions were necessary to protect the identity of a witness. Defendants can consult an attorney and have the right to confront witnesses and challenge evidence against them, present witnesses and evidence on their own behalf, and appeal judgment to a higher court. The law extends these rights to all citizens, and officials did not deny these rights during the year; however, authorities rarely informed detainees of their rights or the reasons for their arrest or detention, according to Amnesty International. Lawyers of accused persons may request access to government-held evidence, but they rarely did so. In cases where the court orders a person who is granted bail to provide a "surety," guarantors deposit their national documents, as required by the court, to facilitate the release of the accused persons on bail. Should the accused jump bail, the guarantors who deposited "sureties" are arrested.

Military tribunals cannot try civilians. A judge advocate presides over court-martial proceedings assisted by a panel of senior military officers. Unlike in previous years, recent proceedings were not open to media or the public. In April 2015 authorities issued a press release announcing the verdict in the trial by court-martial of six persons charged with treason and other offenses related to the failed coup attempt of December 2014. Authorities sentenced Lieutenant Colonel Sarjo Jarju, Lieutenant Buba Sanneh, and former private Modou Njie to death. Captain Abdoulie Jobe, Captain Buba K. Bojang, and Lieutenant Amadou Sowe received life sentences. On April 8, four of the convicts--Jarju, Sowe, Sanneh, and Njie--appealed their verdicts, but on June 10, the High Court dismissed their appeals on the ground it lacked jurisdiction, despite Section 130 (2) of the constitution that provides, "The Court of Appeal shall have jurisdiction in appeals from courts-martial in the manner provided by law."

The judicial system also recognizes customary law and sharia (Islamic law).

Customary law covers marriage and divorce for non-Muslims, inheritance, land tenure, tribal and clan leadership, and other traditional and social relations. District chiefs preside over local tribunals that administer customary law at the district level. Customary law recognizes the rights of all citizens regardless of age, gender, and religion; however, it requires women to show respect for their husbands and children for their parents.

Sharia applies in domestic matters, including Muslim marriage, divorce, and inheritance. Qadi courts and district tribunals do not offer standard legal representation to the parties in a case, since lawyers are not trained in Islamic or customary law.

Political Prisoners and Detainees

During the year there were credible reports the government held civilians based on their political views or associations and held some incommunicado for prolonged periods. Political prisoners at year's end included 30 supporters of the UDP, including the party leader and several executive members. The UDP supporters were arrested following peaceful protests on April 14 and 16 and a peaceful march on May 9. They were convicted on six of seven original charges and sentenced to three years' imprisonment on July 20 and 21. One of those convicted in association with the protests was found guilty, although the judge in the case noted in her written ruling the prosecution had not proved its case against the defendant. Authorities held these prisoners at Mile 2 Prison; by law they were denied visits from family members until three months after the date of conviction. More than 90 days after their arrest, the prisoners had still not been allowed visits by either family members or lawyers at year's end. The government also did not allow international human rights organizations, local NGOs, civil society organizations, or the International Committee of the Red Cross regular access to these detainees. Fourteen UDP supporters, arrested during the peaceful May 9 march from the Banjul High Court to the home of UDP leader Ousainou Darboe, remained in custody and on trial.

Civil Judicial Procedures and Remedies

The High Court has jurisdiction to hear cases concerning civil and human rights violations, although it may decline to exercise its powers if it is satisfied other adequate means of redress are available. The Indemnity Act prevented victims from seeking redress in some cases.

The government failed to comply with several court decisions pertaining to human rights. Several court orders authorizing visits by family members and receipt of food and clothing from outside the prison were ignored by the government in the case of the UDP supporters detained after the April 14 and April 16 peaceful protests. Individuals and organizations may appeal adverse domestic decisions to regional human rights bodies. On August 6, the UDP filed a suit challenging the arbitrary arrest, assault, torture, unfair trial, conviction, and three-year sentence of 30 UDP members at the ECOWAS Court. The UDP was also seeking financial compensation totaling 310 million dalasi ($7.04 million) at the court.

f. Arbitrary or Unlawful Interference with Privacy, Family, Home, or Correspondence

The constitution and law prohibit such actions, but the government did not respect these prohibitions, although it generally enforced Decree 45, which applies constitutional safeguards against arbitrary searches and the seizure of property without due process. Observers believed the government monitored citizens engaged in activities it deemed objectionable.

Section 2. Respect for Civil Liberties, Including:

a. Freedom of Speech and Press

The constitution and law provide for freedom of speech and press; however, the government restricted these rights. The *Freedom in the World 2015* report by Freedom House stated, "The government does not respect freedom of the press. Laws on sedition give authorities discretion in silencing dissent, and independent media outlets and journalists are subject to harassment, arrest, and violence."

Freedom of Speech and Expression: Individuals who publicly or privately criticized the government or the president risked government reprisal.

On May 11, three men--Ebrima Keita, Musa Fofana, and Alasana Jallow--were arrested. They were arraigned before the Bundung Magistrate Court on May 24, charged with seditious intention and incitement of violence. In court the prosecutor claimed the three men were arrested because they said, "All members of the opposition parties should come together and organize a mass demonstration which will make it difficult for the security forces to handle. President Jammeh never liked the Mandinkas." On May 30, the court granted bail to each of the accused in the sum of 50,000 dalasi ($1,140) with two sureties (financial deposits by persons who guarantee the accused will return to court). The matter was still before the court at year's end.

<u>Press and Media Freedoms</u>: Laws that impose excessive bonds on media institutions also require newspapers to reregister annually and mandate harsh punishment for the publication of so-called false information or undermining constitutional protections. According to Freedom House, these provisions gave authorities great power to silence dissent.

The 2013 Information and Communication Act criminalizes the dissemination of "false news" about government or public officials, inciting dissatisfaction or instigating violence against the government, or caricaturing or otherwise making derogatory statements against public officials on the internet. These crimes are punishable by hefty fines or a prison term of up to 15 years or both. Self-censorship among media professionals was common.

In July 2015 NIA officers arrested and detained Alagie Ceesay, managing director of private radio station Taranga FM, for several days at NIA headquarters. Taranga is the only radio station in the country that translates local newspaper articles into local languages, a practice that previously caused friction with authorities. Officials accused Ceesay of sharing by cellphone text a photograph of President Jammeh with a gun and five bullets pointed at his head. The inspector general of police charged Ceesay with "intent to raise discontent, hatred, or disaffection of the president" at the magistrate's court. In August 2015 the director of public prosecution filed six other charges of "sedition and seditious intent" at the High Court, all related to the same photograph. In October 2015 magistrate Momodou Jallow, at the request of a police prosecutor, dismissed the charge against Ceesay, formally ending his trial in the lower court. The courts rejected his bail application four times. On April 22, the state-owned Gambia Radio and Television Services (GRTS) announced Ceesay had escaped on April 20 while undergoing medical treatment at Edward Francis Small Teaching Hospital in Banjul and stated that anyone aiding Ceesay's flight would "face the full force of the law." The case remained unresolved in the High Court at year's end.

The independent *Daily Observer* newspaper favored the government in its coverage and editorials. Four other independent newspapers, including one published by an opposition party, remained highly critical of the government. A 2012 ban on the *Daily News* newspaper remained in force.

GRTS and nine private radio stations broadcast throughout the country. GRTS gave virtually no coverage to political opposition activities but provided extensive coverage of ruling party activities.

<u>Violence and Harassment</u>: Media restrictions remained stringent during the year. Numerous journalists remained in self-imposed exile due to government threats and harassment. While there were no reports of journalists being arrested and detained, human rights organization Article 19 received several reports of journalists receiving threatening phone calls after mentioning information critical of the government published by international media.

Officials routinely denied journalists from news outlets perceived to be critical of the government access to public information and excluded them from covering official events at certain venues.

<u>Censorship or Content Restrictions</u>: Private media outlets generally practiced self-censorship due to fear of reprisal by the government, and many refrained from publishing content deemed contrary to the principles of Islam or offensive to other religions and sects. Nevertheless, opposition views regularly appeared in the independent press, and there was frequent criticism of the government in the English-language private press.

The Information and Communication Act created several new offenses for online speech that are punishable by a 15-year prison term or a fine of three million dalasi ($68,200) or both. The act criminalizes spreading false news about the government or public officials, making caricatures or derogatory statements regarding public officials, and inciting dissatisfaction with or instigating violence against the government.

<u>National Security</u>: Unlike in previous years, the NIA was not involved in the arbitrary closure of media outlets and the extrajudicial detention of journalists. The Gambia Press Union, however, claimed Alagie Ceesay, Radio Taranga FM manager, was tortured while in custody.

Internet Freedom

There were few government restrictions on access to the internet or credible reports the government monitored private online communications without appropriate legal authority. Internet users, however, reported they often could not access the websites of foreign online publications such as Freedom Online.

The Africa Market and Telecommunications Report for 2016 reported 18.6 percent of individuals used the internet during the year. In August the government reportedly restricted public access to Voice Over Internet Protocol services, including Skype and other popular social media applications, such as FaceTime, Facebook video messaging, and WhatsApp. These restrictions did not remain in place at year's end.

Academic Freedom and Cultural Events

In June 2015 hip-hop artist Ali Cham, known as Killa Ace, released a song critical of government actions, particularly its restrictions on free speech and press freedom, police brutality, corruption, and misuse of public funds. The song was available online. Although officials did not ban the song, Cham fled the country with his wife and daughter, saying he no longer felt safe after his parents received threatening inquiries from security officers.

b. Freedom of Peaceful Assembly and Association

Freedom of Assembly

The constitution and law provide for freedom of assembly; however, police systematically refused requests for permission to hold demonstrations, including peaceful ones, and occasionally refused to issue permits to opposition parties wishing to hold rallies.

On April 14, UDP supporters assembled peacefully at Westfield Junction in Serrekunda, the commercial center, and called for "proper electoral reform." The UDP's Youth Wing Leader, Solo Sandeng, who led the protest, was arrested along with an unspecified number of fellow protesters by officers of the Police Intervention Unit (PIU). The PIU reportedly used excessive force to disperse the crowds. Sandeng died in police custody soon after his arrest. UDP leader, Ousainou Darboe, led a peaceful protest march on April 16, demanding the release of Sandeng "dead or alive." Darboe was arrested, along with a relative, Fanta Jawara, a Gambian-American citizen. Members of the UDP executive, and several others were also arrested. The government described the protest as "illegal," on the grounds the demonstrators did not have a police permit, even though the constitution allows for peaceful protests.

In April 2015 officers from the PIU and other security agencies armed with riot gear intercepted a team of officials and supporters of the opposition UDP, including leader Ousainou Darboe. The group arrived at the village of Fass Njaga, Choi, in the North Bank Region, on the first day of a 10-day campaign tour. The UDP decided to embark on the tour despite lacking a police permit for use of a public address system. Under the Public Order Act, political parties planning to hold public meetings must apply for a permit allowing them to use a public address system and must provide details of place, date, and time of each rally. The PIU prevented the UDP team from holding a meeting in Fass Njaga or proceeding on the campaign tour. A tense four-day standoff continued until police finally issued a permit allowing the UDP to continue its tour.

Freedom of Association

The constitution and law provide for freedom of association, and the government generally respected this right in practice.

c. Freedom of Religion

See the Department of State's *International Religious Freedom Report* at www.state.gov/religiousfreedomreport/.

d. Freedom of Movement, Internally Displaced Persons, Protection of Refugees, and Stateless Persons

The constitution and law provide for freedom of movement within the country, foreign travel, emigration, and repatriation, and the government generally respected these rights.

The government cooperated with the Office of the UN High Commissioner for Refugees (UNHCR) and other humanitarian organizations to assist internally displaced persons, refugees, asylum seekers, stateless persons, or other persons of concern. UNHCR coordinated government efforts with the International Organization for Migration, the Gambia Red Cross Society, and other agencies to provide this protection and assistance.

In-country Movement: There are no restrictions on the right to freedom of movement and residence within the borders of the state. Citizens of the ECOWAS do not require visas to enter the country. ECOWAS citizens are also exempt from fees related to entry clearances, emergency travel certificates, and extensions of stay. The government occasionally installed security checkpoints at strategic locations and demanded personal identification documents from individuals.

Foreign Travel: The government imposed restrictions on foreign travel by many persons released from detention, often by confiscating their travel documents temporarily at time of arrest or soon afterward. As a rule the government required all its employees to obtain permission from the Office of the President before traveling abroad on official trips. In 2014 the president signed an amendment to the criminal code that criminalizes the act of absconding while performing government duties abroad. According to the amendment, "A person who leaves The Gambia under a government-sponsored program or on a mission as a representative of The Gambia and refuses to return home on completion of his or her program or mission commits an offense." Conviction could result in a fine of 500,000 dalasi ($11,400) and imprisonment for five years.

Exile: There were no known cases of persons arbitrarily deprived of the right to return to the country. In July 2015 the president extended amnesty to all citizens in the diaspora and said they are forgiven and can freely return home.

In October the government issued travel documents to 11 citizens in foreign custody as a result of the government's refusal to provide travel documents required for their repatriation. The first two detainees arrived in the country on October 25, and the remaining citizens were subsequently returned.

Ousman Sonko, the country's former minister of interior was fired on September 16. Sonko sought political asylum in Sweden on September 22. According to media reports, he was deported from Sweden to Spain, the first EU country he entered on leaving the Gambia, to make his asylum application.

Protection of Refugees

Access to Asylum: The law provides for granting refugee status under the 2008 Refugee Act. The Gambia Commission for Refugees worked with UNHCR on protection of refugees.

UNHCR provided assistance with basic needs and services and implemented livelihood programs. According to UNHCR's resident representative, the approximately 8,000 refugees in the country are largely Senegalese who fled the Casamance conflict in Senegal. In recent years the country has also hosted smaller numbers of refugees from Sierra Leone, Liberia, Togo, the Republic of the Congo, the Democratic Republic of the Congo, Somalia, Eritrea, Sudan, and Guinea-Bissau. UNHCR reported many of these refugees have not returned to their countries of origin.

Section 3. Freedom to Participate in the Political Process

The constitution and law provide the ability of citizens to choose their government in free and fair elections; however, citizens were unable to exercise this ability fully in the 2011 presidential election due to government intimidation of voters and ruling party control of the media. The country held generally peaceful national assembly elections in 2012 and local government elections in 2013. The country has an independent electoral commission (IEC), but the president appoints members in consultation with the Judicial Service Commission and the Public Service Commission. The current members of the commission have all exceeded their terms in office.

Elections and Political Participation

Recent Elections: In 2012 voters elected members of the National Assembly. Six of the seven opposition parties boycotted the voting after the IEC refused to accept demands they had submitted, including for a postponement of the election. President Jammeh's party, the APRC, won 43 seats, the opposition National Reconciliation Party (NRP) one seat, and independent candidates four seats. In August 2015 the NRP won another seat in a by-election in the Lower Saloum constituency, following the president's dismissal of the APRC incumbent, Pa Malick Ceesay.

During local elections in 2013, independent candidates won 10 of the 45 wards in which they competed. The ruling APRC party and the NRP were the only parties that participated. Incumbent mayor of Banjul Samba Faal (APRC) lost to independent candidate Abdoulie Bah by a wide margin. In April 2013, before the election, the APRC expelled Bah from the party, citing "manners incompatible with the Party's code of conduct." Bah then decided to run as an independent and focused on the poor state of roads in Banjul.

Political Parties and Political Participation: The APRC held 42 of 48 elected seats in the National Assembly and continued to maintain tight control over the political landscape. An additional five seats were filled by presidential appointees. APRC membership conferred advantages, such as expediting government transactions, facilitating access to certain documents, and securing employment contracts. There were eight opposition political parties. In May 2015, six opposition political parties jointly presented a set of 13 proposals and demands for electoral and constitutional reforms before the commencement of a new electoral cycle in 2016. Neither the IEC nor the government met with opposition parties to address the proposals before the elections were held. IEC chairman Alieu Momarr Njai addressed one of the 13 concerns when he revitalized the Interparty Committee to serve as a forum for dialogue and cooperation. President Jammeh's statement against members of the Mandinka ethnic group limited their rights for political participation. For example, during a June 3 political rally in Talinding, Kanifing Municipal Council, the president reportedly threatened to kill members of the Mandinka tribe, the country's largest ethnic group (constituting 42 percent of the population). He reportedly said, "I will wipe you out and nothing will come out of it," and "Anybody who dares to demonstrate, go ahead and see what will happen."

Participation of Women and Minorities: Observers noted there were cultural constraints on women's political participation. There were four women in the 53-seat national assembly: three elected and one nominated by the president. At year's end there were five women in the 21-member cabinet, including the vice president. Of 1,873 village heads, only five were women.

No statistics were available on the percentage of ethnic minority members in the legislature or the cabinet. The president and many members of his administration are from the minority Jola ethnic group.

Section 4. Corruption and Lack of Transparency in Government

While the law provides criminal penalties for corruption by officials, the government did not implement the law effectively. The World Bank's most recent *Worldwide Governance Indicators* reflected corruption was a serious problem.

Corruption: There were prosecutions for corruption of several civilian officials during the year. For example, on June 20, the president dismissed 10 former and current senior officials of the Ministry of Petroleum, including former minister Sirra Wally Ndow-Njie, for allegedly appropriating funds from oil contracts. In a July 6 speech, the president stated the Ministry of Petroleum had signed an agreement with a bogus oil company in Dubai that resulted in the loss of 528 million dalasi ($12 million).

Financial Disclosure: The law subjects public officials, both appointed and elected, to financial disclosure laws, but the government seldom enforced these laws. The law mandates no particular agency to monitor and verify disclosures, but the president may appoint judicial commissions of inquiry to investigate any category of public officials or private individuals. The meetings of such commissions were public.

<u>Public Access to Information</u>: The constitution and law do not provide for public access to government information. The law prohibits civil servants from divulging information about their departments or speaking to the press without prior clearance from their department heads.

Section 5. Governmental Attitude Regarding International and Nongovernmental Investigation of Alleged Violations of Human Rights

A number of domestic and international human rights groups operated despite government restrictions, and they were sometimes able to investigate and publish findings on human rights cases. Government officials seldom were cooperative or responsive to their views. The British Home Office *Country Information and Guidance Report on The Gambia* in 2015 stated, "Some human rights activists who have (or have been perceived to have) criticized the government are at risk of being harassed, arrested, detained, intimidated and ill-treated by state agents. Reports note they have faced torture and enforced disappearance."

The 1996 NGO Decree imposes a cumbersome registration process, allows the government to reject NGO registration applications even when formal registration requirements have been met, and requires annual submissions of budgets and work programs. The 2010 decision to place supervision of NGO activities under the Office of the President resulted in increased restrictions. Human rights organizations censored themselves and focused on nonsensitive problems; most human rights NGOs did not actively document or publicly report human rights abuses within the country due to fear of reprisal.

Although the government has often harassed, arrested, and detained human rights workers, there were no known detentions of human rights workers during the year.

<u>The United Nations or Other International Bodies</u>: The government allowed visits related to human rights concerns during the year by the EU and other international governmental organizations, such as ECOWAS. The government offered no public response to reports issued by these organizations after the visits. A delegation from the European Parliament's Subcommittee on Human Rights visited September 19-23. The visit was to gather information, encourage the government to improve its human rights record, and to support human rights campaigners. The delegation met with representatives of the National Assembly, Independent Electoral Commission, Ombudsman, women's associations, and opposition parties. The EU Parliament expressed concern in a May resolution on the government's violent repression of peaceful protests in April; the arrest and

torture of protesters, including leading figures in the UDP; and serious concern about the likelihood of free and fair presidential elections in December. On May 5, an ECOWAS-African Union-UN Joint Mission met with government officials and opposition political parties. The mission reportedly expressed concern about the April 14 and April 16 protesters' arrests, treatment, denial of bail, and lack of access to family members and lawyers.

Government Human Rights Bodies: The Office of the Ombudsman operated a National Human Rights Unit (NHRU) to promote and protect human rights and support vulnerable groups. During the year the unit addressed complaints regarding unlawful dismissal, termination of employment, unfair treatment, and illegal arrest and detention. According to its report presented to the National Assembly on February 3, the Ombudsman's Office received 127 complaints in 2014. Of these, authorities resolved 42 per cent of cases in favor of the complainants, dismissed 22 per cent for lack of merit, and discontinued 12 per cent considered frivolous; 2 per cent of complaints were withdrawn and 23 per cent left pending.

Section 6. Discrimination, Societal Abuses, and Trafficking in Persons

Women

Rape and Domestic Violence: The penalty for rape is life imprisonment; however, rape, including spousal rape, was a widespread problem. The maximum penalty for attempted rape is 10 years' imprisonment without an option of a fine. NGOs involved in advocating against rape and abuse of women suggested that prosecutors often failed to prosecute rape cases aggressively. For example, on September 27, the *Daily Observer* reported police in Upper River Region arrested and detained two boys for allegedly "gang-raping an underage girl." On October 17, Magistrate Hilary Abeke of Kanifing Magistrate Court acquitted and discharged Babucarr Bah on grounds the evidence of the prosecutors was contradictory and doubtful. Bah was standing trial on five charges, ranging from attempted rape, unlawful detention, kidnapping and abduction, and sexual exploitation of a child. Authorities prosecuted at least six rape cases reported to police in 2015; most prosecutions resulted in conviction. The law against spousal rape was difficult to enforce effectively, as many did not consider spousal rape a crime and failed to report it. Police generally considered spousal rape to be a domestic issue outside their jurisdiction.

The law prohibits any form of violence against women, and stipulates a fine of 50,000 dalasi ($1,140) or imprisonment not exceeding two years, or both. Victims underreported domestic violence due to social stigma, and victims settled most cases through family mediation. No statistics were available on abusers prosecuted or convicted. The government developed a national plan of action on gender-based violence (GBV) for 2013-17, with the goal of reducing the percentage of women who experience GBV from 75 percent to 30 percent. The *Gambia 2013 Demographic and Health Survey*, published in 2015, stated the percentage of women who reported having experienced GBV fell to 41 percent during 2013.

The Gambia Committee on Traditional Practices Affecting the Health of Women and Children (GAMCOTRAP), one of the leading women's rights NGOs in the country, included GBV in its training modules for combating FGM/C. Another group, the Female Lawyers' Association of The Gambia, educated women on their rights and represented them, often without charge, in domestic violence cases.

Female Genital Mutilation/Cutting (FGM/C): In December 2015 the National Assembly passed the Women's Amendment Act of 2015, which banned FGM/C. The new law stipulates imprisonment for not more than three years, a fine of 50,000 dalasi ($1,140), or both, for anyone found to have circumcised a female child. It also states a life sentence may be applicable in instances where the practice results in death of the victim. Accomplices who are aware of the practice but fail to report it may be liable for a fine of 10,000 dalasi ($227). On March 10, Banjul Magistrate Court charged two women with four criminal offenses, after a five-month-old girl child died of FGM/C in the Kiang West, Sankandi village, Lower River Region (LRR). The accused, Sunkaru Darboe, and Saffiatou Darboe, denied the allegations. On March 21, the Banjul Magistrate Court transferred the case to Mansankonko High Court in LRR for lack of jurisdiction. The case remained pending at year's end.

In a 2005-06 survey, the UN Children's Fund (UNICEF) found almost 80 percent of girls and women between ages 15 and 19 in the country had undergone FGM/C, and seven of the nine major ethnic groups practiced FGM/C on girls from shortly after birth until age 16. Type 2, the partial or total removal of the clitoris and the labia minora, with or without excision of the labia majora, was the most prevalent. FGM/C was less frequent among educated and urban groups. Some religious leaders, such as the State House imam, Muhammed Lamin Touray, publicly defended the practice.

There were reports of health complications, including deaths, associated with FGM/C; however, no accurate statistics were available. Several NGOs including GAMCOTRAP conducted public education programs to discourage the practice and spoke out against FGM/C in the media. In 2015 several district chiefs, ward councilors, members of councils of elders, religious leaders, female leaders, and female circumcisers attended GAMCOTRAP seminars on the harmful effects of FGM/C. On February 3, GAMCOTRAP celebrated "International Zero Tolerance to FGM Day" to strengthen awareness-raising and advocacy activities, and to spread information on the universal ban on FGM and its implications at the community and national levels.

Sexual Harassment: The law prohibits sexual harassment and provides for a one-year mandatory prison sentence for offenders. According to GAMCOTRAP, although citizens considered sexual harassment a common problem in workplaces and schools, few reported it to police.

Reproductive Rights: The government did not interfere with the basic right of couples and individuals to decide the number, spacing, and timing of their children; manage their reproductive health; and have the information and means to do so free from discrimination, coercion, or violence. According to the Health Ministry, the maternal mortality rate in 2015 was 360 per 100,000 live births. According to the World Health Organization, hemorrhage, anemia, early pregnancy, and obstructed labor were the main causes of maternal mortality. World Development Indicators published by the World Bank in September 2015 stated the contraceptive prevalence rate for girls and women ages 15 to 49 was 13.3 percent.

Discrimination: The constitution provides for equality for women in the political, economic, and social spheres. The law provides equal rights to men and women, and prohibits discrimination on grounds of gender. The constitution, however, states its provisions against discrimination do not apply to adoption, marriage, divorce, burial, or devolution of property on death, and women experienced a wide range of discrimination in matrimonial, property, and inheritance rights.

Employment in the formal sector was open to women at the same salary rates as men, and no statutory discrimination existed in other kinds of employment (see section 7.d.), access to credit, owning and managing a business, or in housing or education. Societal discrimination, however, lingered in the above areas, and businesses generally employed women in such pursuits as food vending and subsistence farming.

Sharia applies in marriage, divorce, and inheritance cases for Muslims, who make up more than 90 percent of the population. Women can have access to land only through marriage and can only borrow, not inherit, land from their husbands. Women normally received a lower proportion of other assets distributed through inheritance than men did. The respective churches and the Office of the Attorney General settled civil marriage and divorce issues affecting Christians.

Families often arranged marriages. Some ethnic groups practiced polygyny. Women in polygynous unions had problems with property and other rights arising from their marriages. They had the option to divorce but no legal right to disapprove or receive advance notification of subsequent marriages by their husbands. The Women's Bureau under the Office of the Vice President oversees programs to provide for the legal rights of women. Active women's rights groups existed.

Children

Birth Registration: Children derive citizenship by birth within the country's territory or through either parent; however, not all parents registered births. To access care at public health centers, authorities required children to have a clinic card, which was available without birth registration. Authorities often required birth certificates for children to enroll in school, and parents could easily obtain them.

Education: The constitution and law mandate compulsory, tuition-free primary education between the ages of six and 12. In 2014 the government announced plans to make school tuition free for all students in upper basic schools by 2014-15 and for senior secondary schools in 2015-16, with external grant assistance from the World Bank and the Global Partnership for Education. Authorities implemented both changes by September 2015. Under the tuition-free primary education plan, however, families often still have to pay fees for books, uniforms, lunch, school fund contributions, and examination fees.

In 2015 an estimated 75 percent of primary school-age children enrolled in primary schools. Islamic schools (madrassahs) enrolled another 15 percent. Girls constituted approximately half of primary school students and a third of high school students. The enrollment of girls was lower in rural areas, where poverty and cultural factors often led parents to decide against sending daughters to school.

<u>Child Abuse</u>: There were occasional reported cases of child abuse. Authorities generally enforced the law when cases of child abuse or mistreatment came to their attention and imposed criminal penalties in serious cases.

The penalty for rape is life imprisonment. The penalty for both "defilement" and "having carnal knowledge" of a minor child is 14 years' imprisonment.

In January 2015 the High Court sentenced Mama Mbaye to seven years' imprisonment with hard labor for his attempted rape of a four-year-old girl. The offense took place in 2013 in Brufut village, West Coast Region.

In 2014 police in Upper River Region arrested and detained a 35-year-old man, known by the initials "S. C.," for allegedly raping a 10-year-old girl. The accused person was remanded at Janjanbureh Prison, and the case was pending before the High Court in Basse at year's end.

<u>Early and Forced Marriage</u>: Carnal knowledge with a girl under the age of 16 is a felony except within marriage, which can occur as early as age 12. The constitution states, "marriage shall be based on the free and full consent of the intended parties," although in many villages, girls reportedly were forced to marry at a young age. On May 31, the Ministry of Health and Social Welfare issued a press release urging the public to participate in a nationwide "End Child Marriage Campaign," which commenced on June 7. The campaign was intended to create awareness and advocacy on issues related to early child marriages and support national policy action on the protection of human rights, especially addressing violence against girls and women. The campaign also sought to support prosecution of perpetrators of early child marriages. On July 21, deputies at the National Assembly enacted and passed into law the Children's (Amendment) Act 2016 to criminalize child marriage. The newly enacted law provides that any person who contravenes the law is liable for conviction and imprisonment not exceeding 20 years, without the option of a fine. The Children's (Amendment) Act 2016 defined a child as "a person who has not attained maturity and is under the age of 18 years," and described child marriage as "a marriage contracted between a child and an adult or between a child and another child."

According to UNICEF's 2010 multiple indicator report, 8.6 percent of women married before they were 15 years old, while 46.5 percent married before the age of 18. The government worked in conjunction with NGO Tostan and UNICEF on a joint community empowerment program seeking the abandonment of early and forced marriage.

Female Genital Mutilation/Cutting (FGM/C): This information is provided in the women's section above.

Sexual Exploitation of Children: The law provides for 14 years' imprisonment for commercial sexual exploitation of children and five years for involvement in child pornography. The constitution provides that children under age 16 be protected from economic exploitation and hazardous employment harmful to their health or physical, mental, spiritual, moral, or social development. The minimum age for consensual sex is 18 years. Local NGOs believed criminals exploited children, who were often seeking to support their families, in prostitution in some brothels and that tourists staying in remote guesthouses and motels were involved in the sexual exploitation of children. Authorities instructed security officers in the tourism development area to turn away all minors who approached the main resort areas without an acceptable reason. NGOs reported difficulties in moving reports of sexual exploitation of children from communities to police, and from police to the courts, and in both the communities and the courts. NGOs largely blamed many of the difficulties on a national culture of secrecy with regard to intimate family issues and a penchant for resolution outside of the formal system.

International Child Abductions: The country is not a party to the 1980 Hague Convention on the Civil Aspects of International Child Abduction. For information see the Department of State's report on compliance at travel.state.gov/content/childabduction/en/legal/compliance.html.

Anti-Semitism

There was no known Jewish community, and there were no reports of anti-Semitic acts.

Trafficking in Persons

See the Department of State's *Trafficking in Persons Report* at www.state.gov/j/tip/rls/tiprpt/.

Persons with Disabilities

The constitution prohibits discrimination against or exploitation of persons with disabilities, although it does not expressly reference the kinds of disabilities protected, particularly as regards access to health services, education, and employment (see section 7.d.). Authorities effectively enforced these provisions. There is no explicit legal guarantee of access to air travel and other transportation, nor any requirement to provide for access to buildings for persons with disabilities. Very few public buildings in the country were accessible to them. The laws do not explicitly prohibit discrimination against persons with physical, sensory, intellectual, or mental disabilities. No laws or programs stipulate persons with disabilities should have access to information or communications. The law requires judicial proceedings involving a person with disabilities take into account the disabilities.

Persons with severe disabilities experienced discrimination and subsisted primarily through private charity. Persons with less severe disabilities encountered less discrimination, including in employment for which they were physically and mentally capable.

The Department of Social Welfare of the Ministry of Health is responsible for protecting the rights of persons with disabilities and worked with the Gambia Organization for the Visually Impaired and the School for the Deaf and Blind to help educate children with disabilities and to develop relevant skills. Most children with disabilities, however, did not attend school. The department also worked with international donors to supply wheelchairs to some persons with disabilities. Several NGOs sought to improve awareness of the rights of persons with disabilities and encouraged their participation in sports and other physical activities. The NHRU, a unit of the Office of the Ombudsman, sought to promote the rights of women with disabilities. Persons with disabilities received priority access to polling booths on election days.

Indigenous People

During the year there were reports the government did not effectively protect the civil, political, and economic rights of indigenous people. President Jammeh's reported inflammatory remarks in a June campaign rally aimed at the large Mandinka ethnic community (see Section 3 above) provoked a strong response from the UN special adviser on the prevention of genocide. On June 10, he stated that such "vitriolic rhetoric" had historically been "both a warning sign and a powerful trigger for atrocity crimes."

Acts of Violence, Discrimination, and Other Abuses Based on Sexual Orientation and Gender Identity

In 2014 the president signed into law an amendment to the criminal code making "aggravated homosexuality" a crime punishable by life imprisonment. The bill defines "aggravated homosexuality" to include serial offenders or persons with a previous conviction for homosexual activity, persons having same-sex relations with someone under the age of 18 or with members of other vulnerable groups, or a person with HIV having same-sex relations.

Prior to this amendment, the law established prison terms ranging from five to 14 years for any man who commits in public or private "any act of gross indecency," engages a male sex worker, or has actual sexual contact with another man. There was no similar law applicable to women. Antidiscrimination laws do not protect lesbian, gay, bisexual, transgender, or intersex (LGBTI) individuals.

In 2014 the NIA arrested three persons on suspicion of homosexual activities, following a security operation targeting persons suspected of being involved in illegal activity. The men--Alieu Sarr, Momarr Sowe, and M. L. Bittaye--appeared before a magistrate in Banjul in 2014. The group was the first authorities tried under the "aggravated homosexuality" amendment. Authorities later transferred the case to the High Court, and in July 2015 the court acquitted Sarr and Sowe. They thereafter left the country. The trial of the third accused, M. L. Bittaye, was in progress at year's end. On April 27, defense counsel Borry Touray filed and submitted a "no case to answer" plea to the High Court, on the ground the state failed to produce any witness to testify against the accused. The trial judge ordered the state to respond to the "no case to answer" submission. As of year's end, this case remained pending before the court.

There were reports of LGBTI citizens fleeing to neighboring countries due to fear of arrest.

There was strong societal discrimination against LGBTI individuals. There were no LGBTI organizations in the country.

HIV and AIDS Social Stigma

Societal discrimination against persons infected with HIV/AIDS hindered identification and treatment of persons with the disease and resulted in their rejection by partners and relatives when their condition became known. The government took a multisectoral approach to fighting HIV/AIDS through its national strategic plan, which provided for care, treatment, and support for persons with or affected by HIV/AIDS. The plan, enacted in 2015, also included HIV-prevention programs for high-risk populations. The Global Fund maintains a 739 million dalasi ($16.8 million) HIV/AIDs program for the country for the period from July 2015 to December 2017. The National AIDs Secretariat (NAS), a government institution, is expected to implement the curative aspect of the program, and Action Aid The Gambia (AATG), an international NGO, is expected to execute the preventive part of the program. There were no reports on HIV-related stigma and discrimination in employment, housing, or access to education or health care.

Section 7. Worker Rights

a. Freedom of Association and the Right to Collective Bargaining

The Labor Act provides that workers, except for civil servants, domestic workers, and certain other categories of workers excluded from the protection of the law, are free to form and join independent unions, conduct legal strikes, and bargain collectively. Military personnel, police officers, other civil service employees, and domestic workers are prohibited from forming unions or going on strike. Additionally, the law authorizes the minister responsible for labor matters to exclude any other category of workers from the protection of the Labor Act. Unions must register to be recognized. The law requires a minimum membership of 50 workers for the registration of a trade union. The law also provides that the registrar of unions may examine without cause the financial accounts of workers' associations.

The law restricts the right to strike by requiring unions to give the commissioner of labor written notice 14 days before beginning an industrial action (28 days for actions involving essential services). Police and military personnel had access to a complaints unit, and civil servants could take their complaints to the public service commission or the government's personnel management office. An employer may apply to a court for an injunction to prohibit industrial action deemed to be in pursuit of a political objective. The court also may forbid action judged to be in breach of a collectively agreed procedure for settlement of industrial disputes. The law prohibits retribution against strikers who comply with the law regulating strikes. Employers may not fire or discriminate against members of registered unions for engaging in legal union activities, and the law provides for reinstatement of workers fired for union activity. The law also sets minimum contract standards for hiring, training, and terms of employment and provides that contracts may not prohibit union membership. Lack of enforcement of the labor law contributed to persistent violations. There are no separate regulations supporting the labor law. Although there were minimal contentious union activities or labor disputes, the government generally did not effectively enforce the law. Resources, inspections, and remediation were inadequate.

The government generally respected freedom of association and the right to collective bargaining for those covered by the Labor Act. Worker organizations were independent of the government and political parties. There were, however, instances of government interference in union activities, including the targeted dissolving of unions. For example, on January 25, the government banned The Gambia National Transport Control Association (GNTCA) from any involvement in the transportation sector in the country. All GNTCA structures, controls, systems, and tariffs (not approved by the government) were dismantled, dissolved, and abolished. The government urged all actors in goods transportation and trading activities to channel their transactions through The Gambia Revenue Authority. On February 21, the secretary general of the banned GNTCA, Sheriff Dibba, died at a medical facility while in custody. Dibba and eight GNTCA executive members had been arrested and charged with economic crimes. The executives were released on court bail following Dibba's death. There were no cases in which authorities denied registration to a union that had applied. There were no other reported incidents of violence, threats, or other abuses targeting union leaders or members by government or employers.

Although trade unions were small and fragmented, collective bargaining took place. Unions were able to negotiate without government interference; however, they lacked experience, organization, and professionalism and often turned to the government for assistance in negotiations. Collective bargaining, arbitration, or agreements reached between unions and management determined union members' wages, which generally exceeded legal minimums. The Department of Labor registered most collective agreements, which remained valid for three years, after which they could be renewed.

The government intervened to assist workers whose employers had fired or discriminated against them. For example, in 2015 the Department of Labor and the Gambia Workers Union supported the case of 30 Capital Gas employees alleging wrongful termination by the company. Complaints also included nonpayment of overtime, annual leave, and nonpayment of social security. Capital Gas agreed to a settlement in which it paid its former employees 1.15 million dalasi ($26,100).

There were no reports of violations of collective bargaining rights or of employers refusing to bargain, bargaining with unions not chosen by workers, or using other hiring practices to avoid hiring workers with bargaining rights.

b. Prohibition of Forced or Compulsory Labor

The constitution and law prohibit all forms of forced or compulsory labor, including that of children, but the government did not effectively enforce these laws.

Officials took part in a number of programs designed to increase their sensitivity to the problem and educate them on ways to investigate and combat it, but child labor continued to occur. Women and children were primary targets subjected to trafficking and commercial sexual exploitation. Inadequate resources made enforcement difficult. While the Labor Act does not specifically prohibit slavery or forced labor, it sets forth general employment protections, including contractual rights, freedom of association, the right to collective bargaining, and disciplinary procedures in the workplace, among other important labor regulations. Penalties were insufficient to deter violations.

Trafficking in persons is a serious problem; trafficking victims usually end up as street vendors, sex workers, and domestic servants. The country is a source and destination for women and children subjected to forced labor and sex trafficking. Criminals subjected women, girls, and, to a lesser extent, boys to sex trafficking and domestic servitude. The government did not fully comply with the minimum standards for the elimination of trafficking and did not make significant efforts to do so.

During the year police and social workers did not report any incidents of Quranic teachers, known as "marabouts," forcing their students, known as "almudus," to sell items on the streets. The practice had become rare since police intervened and ordered marabouts to stop the practice.

In August 2015 the state-owned television station broadcast appeals for volunteers to provide free labor at President Jammeh's private farms. The secretary general in the Office of the President, Lamin Nyabally, issued a circular to civil servants instructing all heads of departments, ministries, and state-owned enterprises to take their staff to the president's home village of Kanilai to work on his farms. According to several reports, there was an expectation communities and government workers would participate. The government reportedly withheld state resources from villages that did not work. Civil servants allegedly understood their jobs depended on committing to this annual call for compulsory labor.

See also the Department of State's *Trafficking in Persons Report* at www.state.gov/j/tip/rls/tiprpt/.

c. Prohibition of Child Labor and Minimum Age for Employment

The constitution prohibits economic exploitation of children under age 16, and regulations prohibit children under 18 years from engaging in exploitive labor or hazardous employment, including mining and quarrying, going to sea, carrying heavy loads, operating heavy machinery, and working in establishments serving alcohol. The Children's Act sets the minimum age at 16 for light work and at 12 for apprenticeship in the informal sector.

The Department of Labor is responsible for enforcing child labor laws and conventions on the worst forms of child labor, but it did not effectively do so. The government took no action to prevent or combat child labor during the year. The labor commissioner registered employee labor cards, which include a person's age; the law authorizes the commissioner to enforce child labor laws. The Labor Act establishes penalties of imprisonment for up to five years and a fine of 100,000 dalasi ($2,270) for violations related to the employment of children. The Children's Act also establishes penalties of imprisonment and fines for any person who contravenes the provisions related to child labor. Enforcement inspections rarely took place.

Child labor in the informal sector was difficult to regulate. Rising school fees combined with stagnating incomes prevented some families from sending their children to school, contributing to child labor. In urban areas some children worked as street vendors, domestic laborers, or taxi and bus assistants. There were a few instances of children begging on the streets. Children between the ages of 14 and 17 also worked in carpentry, masonry, plumbing, tailoring, and auto repair. Children in rural areas worked on family farms.

Implementation of the Children's Act and prosecution of suspected offenders also remained infrequent. Penalties for violations (including minimum terms of imprisonment for the offense of trafficking in persons from 15 to 50 years of age) were insufficient to deter violations.

See also the Department of Labor's *Findings on the Worst Forms of Child Labor* at www.dol.gov/ilab/reports/child-labor/findings.

d. Discrimination with Respect to Employment and Occupation

The constitution prohibits discrimination based on race, color, gender, language, religion, political or other opinion, national or social origin, disability, sex, property, birth, or other status.

Employment in the formal sector was open to women at the same salary rates as men, and no statutory discrimination existed in other kinds of employment; however, societal discrimination lingered, and women generally worked in such pursuits as food vending and subsistence farming. The law also prohibits discrimination in private companies certified by the Department of Labor (see section 6).

There were no reports of discriminatory practices with respect to employment or occupation. The International Labor Organization reported the government generally supported elimination of employment discrimination. The laws define the criteria that prohibit discrimination with respect to employment and occupation, and the government effectively enforced the law. Under the Labor Act, a person who commits an offense is liable on conviction to a fine not exceeding 50,000 dalasi ($1,140) for each offense. The penalties appeared to be sufficient to deter violations.

Migrant workers enjoy the same legal protections, wages, and working conditions as citizens.

e. Acceptable Conditions of Work

The minimum wage was 50 dalasi ($1.14) per day, although this applied only to the 20 percent of the workforce employed in the formal sector. The government considered the national poverty baseline to be 38 dalasi ($0.86) per person per day. Employers paid most workers above the minimum wage. The Department of Labor is responsible for enforcing the minimum wage. A majority of workers was employed in the private sector or was self-employed, often in agriculture. Most citizens did not live on a single worker's earnings and shared resources within extended families.

The basic legal workweek is 48 hours within a period not to exceed six consecutive days. The government's workweek included four 10-hour workdays (Monday through Thursday) with schools open on Friday, while the private sector typically operated from Monday through Saturday. There are no limits on hours worked per week and no prohibition of excessive compulsory overtime. Regulations mandate a 30-minute lunch break. Regulations entitle government employees to one month of paid annual leave after one year of service. The government did not pay most government employees overtime compensation. Government workers holding temporary positions and private-sector workers, however, received overtime pay calculated per hour. Private-sector employees received between 14 and 30 days of paid annual leave, depending on length of service. There was no exception for foreign or migrant workers.

The law specifies the safety equipment an employer must provide to employees working in designated occupations. The law also authorizes the Department of Labor to regulate factory health and safety, accident prevention, and dangerous trades and to appoint inspectors to provide for compliance with occupational safety and health standards. Workers may demand protective equipment and clothing for hazardous workplaces and have recourse to the labor department. The law protects foreign workers employed by the government; however, it provides protection for privately employed foreigners only if they have a valid work permit.

The Department of Labor effectively enforced the wage law and workweek standards when workers brought cases to its attention.

In May 2015 one of the trade union umbrella organizations, the Gambia Labor Congress, repeated its call on the government "to effect a general salary review in both the public and private sectors," pointing out skyrocketing inflation was causing hardship in many families. The Ministry of Trade, Industry, Regional Cooperation, and Employment had not responded to the demands as of year's end.

There was no specific government action during the year to prevent violations of workers' rights or to improve working conditions, particularly for hazardous sectors or vulnerable groups.

The law does not provide for workers to remove themselves from situations that endangered health or safety without jeopardy to their employment, and authorities did not effectively protect employees in this situation.